COLE'S COOKING
COMPANION SERIES

W9-BNT-951

PASTA
PERFECT

COLE GROUP

© 1995 Cole Group, Inc.

Front cover photograph: Joyce Oudkerk Pool
Page 5: KitchenAid Portable Appliances, St. Joseph, Michigan 49085
Page 11: Cuisinart (Cuisinart® is a registered trademark of Cuisinart, Stamford, Connecticut 06904)

Cole Group, Inc.
1330 N. Dutton Ave., Suite 103
Santa Rosa, CA 95401
(800) 959-2717   (707) 526-2682
FAX (707) 526-2687

Printed in Hong Kong

G	F	E	D	C	B	A
1	0	9	8	7	6	5

ISBN 1-56426-802-0
Library of Congress Catalog Card Number 94-40117

Distributed to the book trade by Publishers Group West

CONTENTS

Getting Started

*P*asta in all its forms has graced tables in Italy and indeed all over the globe for thousands of years. Perpetually one of the world's most beloved foods, pasta possesses qualities that quite possibly will make it the twenty-first century's food of choice: Pasta's superior nutritional benefits have earned it superfood status. It's also the ideal staple: economical, convenient to store and prepare, and versatile, not to mention highly pleasurable to eat. If there's a perfect food, it's probably pasta.

Pasta, Fresh and Dried

Pasta is made from grain combined with liquid (and sometimes with other ingredients for flavoring or coloring). Kneading produces a smooth dough or paste (hence the word *pasta*) that can be rolled out and cut or formed into any of hundreds of varieties. Making sense out of the multitude of pasta varieties is simplified by dividing pasta into two categories: fresh and dried.

The basic ingredients of *fresh pasta* (see page 8) are flour and eggs, with perhaps a little oil or water added to make the dough easier to work and some salt for flavor. Most commercially produced *dried pasta* (see page 10) is made from only water and semolina, a special variety of flour ground from high-protein durum wheat. Semolina creates a firm, elastic dough that is sturdy enough to be shaped by machine. It can also be used in homemade pasta, either by itself or mixed with all-purpose flour, to strengthen the dough and enhance the texture of the finished product. Unless specified, all the pasta dough recipes in this book can be made with all-purpose flour, semolina, or a blend of the two.

Shopping for Pasta

Look for fresh pasta in specialty stores, Italian markets, and some supermarkets; many stores also stock fresh pasta that has been frozen. Basic dried varieties such as spaghetti, lasagne, and macaroni are easy to find; other traditional Italian varieties as well as novelty shapes and popular "designer" pastas flaunting surprising colors and unusual flavors are available in specialty stores, Italian markets, some supermarkets, and by mail order.

Storing Pasta

Fresh pasta is perishable. It will keep in the refrigerator, wrapped airtight, for about five days, or in the freezer for up to one month (after that it becomes dry and brittle).

Dried pasta will keep almost indefinitely if stored in a cool, dry place in an airtight container or tightly closed package. Leftover cooked dried pasta that is unsauced can be lightly tossed with oil and refrigerated for one or two days. Reheat briefly in boiling water or add to soups.

Cooking Fresh and Dried Pasta

The subtle flavor of pasta makes the quality of the texture especially important. Properly cooked pasta should offer slight resistance to the tooth (al dente), without being soft or mushy.

For each pound (450 g) of pasta, bring about 4 quarts (3.6 l) of water to a rapid boil. Add a little salt, drop the pasta in all at once, stir, and cover the pot until the water returns to a boil; then uncover and boil until pasta is al dente. Fresh pasta generally cooks in 60–90 seconds; dried pasta may take 5 minutes or more, depending on its shape and age. Cook frozen pasta by dropping it directly into boiling water; do not thaw before cooking.

Drain cooked pasta immediately in a colander, shaking to drain off excess cooking water (reserve a little of the cooking water); then pour pasta into a warm bowl. Add olive oil, butter, or sauce and toss. If the pasta seems too thick or dry, add a bit of the reserved cooking water to moisten. Serve immediately.

Pasta that is to be sauced and baked should be undercooked slightly; otherwise it will be too soft after baking. Drain well and toss with a little of the reserved cooking water to keep pasta from sticking together. One pound of uncooked pasta yields about 5 to 6 cups (1.1–1.4 l) cooked and drained pasta. Amounts may vary somewhat, depending upon the variety of pasta. *Wherever pasta is included in a recipe in this book, the quantity listed refers to uncooked pasta unless otherwise stated.*

Fresh Pasta Varieties

If the names for Italian pasta varieties seem confusing, it's because different regions have given different names to the same type of pasta. Here are some of the most common types of fresh pasta:

Agnolotti Crescent-shaped dumplings, usually stuffed with meat or pesto.

Cannelloni Flat rectangles of pasta, usually about 3 by 4 inches (7.5 by 10 cm), that can be stuffed, rolled into tubular "channels," then sauced and baked.

Fettuccine The favorite flat ribbon pasta of Rome, about ⅛ inch (.3 cm) wide; often served with cream sauces.

Gnocchi Chewy dumplings prepared with potato, flour, or polenta.

Lasagne The broadest fresh pasta (also available dried), about 2 inches (5 cm) wide. Cooked lasagne is layered with vegetables, cheeses, sauce (meat, cream, or tomato), and baked.

Maltagliati Triangular or diamond-shaped pasta formed by cutting rolled pasta on the diagonal; typically used in soup.

Pappardelle One of the widest fresh noodles, cut about ⅝ inch (1.3 cm) wide with a fluted pastry cutter to give it a frilly edge; traditionally served with rich meat sauces.

Ravioli, raviolini Squares about 2 inches (5 cm) wide or smaller, served open (flat) or stuffed with a savory or sweet filling.

Tagliarini Long flat ribbons, rolled paper-thin, and cut less than ⅛ inch (.3 cm) wide; often used in broth.

Tagliatelle Similar to fettuccine but slightly thinner and wider, slightly less than ¼ inch (.6 cm) wide; often tossed with rich meat sauces.

Tortellini Small squares filled with meat, vegetables, or cheese, then folded and twisted into ring-shaped dumplings. Cooked tortellini often are added to beef or chicken broth, tossed with butter or olive oil, or combined with sauce (cream or cheese).

Dried Pasta Varieties

Some of the finest dried pasta is manufactured and exported all over the world from factories in southern Italy. Of the hundreds of dried pasta shapes, these are the most commonly available:

Capelli d'Angelo Angel hair pasta, similar to fine spaghetti.

Conchiglie Ridged shells resembling conch shells.

Farfelle, fiochetti Butterflies or bowties; flat pasta about ¾ by 2 inches (1.9 by 5 cm), pinched together in the middle.

Fusilli Spaghetti-length spiral pasta.

Linguine Flat ribbon pasta similar to fettuccine but wider; also available fresh.

Lumache Shells larger than conchiglie (see above) and intended for stuffing with cheese or other fillings.

Macaroni Short, elbow-shaped, hollow pasta. Macaroni (spelled *maccheroni*) is also the generic Italian word for dried pasta.

Manicotti Large "muffs" with ridges, usually stuffed with cheese or meat mixtures, then sauced and baked.

Pastina Assorted tiny pasta shapes used in broth or soup.

Penne Also known as mostaccioli ("mustaches"); quill-like tubes about 2 inches (5 cm) long, cut diagonally on the ends.

Rigatoni Ridged, hollow tubes about ½ by 2 inches (1.25 by 5 cm).

Rotelle Short, 2-inch-long (5-cm), corkscrew-shaped pasta.

Ruote Wheel-shaped pasta; often served in soups.

Spaghetti, spaghettini The familiar rodlike pasta.

Vermicelli Longer, finer, and more fragile than spaghetti; often wound into loose "nests" for ease of handling.

Ziti Long hollow rods the length of spaghetti but slightly thicker. Sometimes ziti are cut into shorter lengths about 2 inches (5 cm) long.

EQUIPMENT FOR MAKING FRESH PASTA

Few pastas you can buy anywhere can compare to the flavor and texture of your own homemade fresh pasta (see pages 19–21). Mixing and kneading pasta dough by hand can be satisfying and fun, although the right equipment makes the job easier and quicker.

Kitchen mixers and food processors can be used to mix ingredients for pasta dough, and, depending on the model, some can also knead and shape the dough. Hand-cranked and electric pasta machines with adjustable metal or plastic rollers are designed to knead, roll out, and cut the dough. Some models can produce both flat and tubular pasta. Automatic pasta makers, like the one shown above, are the ultimate in convenience, making mixing, kneading, and extruding the dough nearly effortless. For more information on using machines to make pasta, see pages 19–20.

Recipes and Techniques for Perfect Pasta

*I*n traditional Italian cuisine, pasta is often presented as a separate course, whereas in the U.S. and elsewhere, pasta may be served as a mealtime opener of soup or salad, as a side dish or main course, or even for dessert. This section showcases the versatility of pasta, with more than 50 recipes and the basic techniques needed for preparing pasta to perfection.

PASTA DOUGHS AND SAUCES

Becoming a master of pasta is a matter of learning how to produce a delightful union of ingredients with different flavors, aromas, colors, and textures. Fresh pasta and sauces made from good-quality ingredients are essential components of all great pasta dishes. On the following pages are recipes and techniques for preparing basic doughs and sauces, as well as ideas for imaginative variations.

PASTA DOUGHS

The delicate flavor and soft texture of fresh pasta you make yourself can't be matched by most commercially manufactured varieties. Another advantage of fresh pasta is that it cooks very quickly (see page 7). Eggs (and sometimes a very little water or oil) provide the only moisture in dough for fresh pasta and make the dough softer and easier to knead and roll out than a flour-and-water dough.

BASIC EGG DOUGH

Once you master this basic recipe, you can use it as the basis for many flavorful, colorful variations of fresh pasta, including your own "designer" varieties (see page 17).

1½ cups	unbleached flour	350 ml
1 tsp	salt	1 tsp
2	eggs, lightly beaten	2

Mix flour and salt in a bowl until blended. Then proceed according to directions for Making Fresh Pasta (see pages 19–21).

Makes 1¼ pounds (570 g) pasta.

ADJUSTING FLOUR AND LIQUID IN DOUGH

The moisture content of pasta dough is affected by a number of variables, including the type of wheat used, the age of the flour, its moisture content, and the degree of humidity in the air. For this reason, even when you measure the ingredients very carefully, you may need to adjust the proportions of flour and liquid if the dough seems too sticky or too dry to handle. Also keep in mind that dough for filled pasta varieties will need to be more moist than dough for flat or tubular pasta. As necessary, add flour or water (no more than ½ teaspoon water or 1 tablespoon flour at a time) until the dough is the proper consistency for rolling and cutting or shaping.

Lemon Dough

Serve this zesty pasta with roast chicken, steamed mussels, or seafood sauces (see page 26). Use only the bright yellow rind of the lemon; the white pith is bitter.

1 recipe	Basic Egg Dough (see page 15)	1 recipe
2 tsp	grated lemon rind	2 tsp
¼ cup	lemon juice	60 ml

Prepare Basic Egg Dough, blending eggs with lemon rind and juice. Proceed according to directions for Making Fresh Pasta (see pages 19–21).

Makes 1¼ pounds (570 g) pasta.

Spinach Dough

Use this dough to make spinach fettuccine, lasagne, or ravioli. Classic Bolognese Sauce (see page 25) complements the flavor and color of spinach pasta. Squeeze as much moisture as possible out of the spinach or the dough will be too wet.

1 recipe	Basic Egg Dough (see page 15)	1 recipe
¾ lb	fresh spinach, blanched, drained, squeezed dry, and finely minced	350 g

Prepare Basic Egg Dough, blending spinach with eggs. Proceed according to directions for Making Fresh Pasta (see pages 19–21).

Makes 1¼ pounds (570 g) pasta.

FRESH HERB DOUGH

Basil, chervil, marjoram, and other fresh herbs can turn Basic Egg Dough into a fragrant pasta that's delicious with just a little olive oil and cheese. Use stronger-flavored herbs such as rosemary and oregano in small quantities, rounding out the cup of herbs called for in the recipe with mild-tasting parsley.

| 1 recipe | Basic Egg Dough (see page 15) | 1 recipe |
| 1 cup | mixed fresh herbs, loosely packed | 1 cup |

Combine flour and salt. Mince herbs, combine with beaten egg, and proceed according to directions for Making Fresh Pasta (see pages 19–21).

Makes 1¼ pounds (570 g) pasta.

DESIGNER DOUGHS

Using Basic Egg Dough (see page 15) as a foundation, you can add different ingredients to create your own "designer" pastas with exciting colors and flavors. Experiment to your heart's (and your palate's) content. Just remember that the color and flavor of the pasta you make should complement whatever sauce you plan to serve with it. Depending on which of the following ingredients you add, you may need to adjust the proportions of liquid and flour to form a dough of proper consistency.

- *Puréed vegetables: cooked beets, roasted red or green bell peppers, cooked pumpkin*

- *Fresh puréed garlic*

- *Spices and seasonings: black pepper, cayenne, cinnamon, chili powder, curry, nutmeg, saffron*

- *Fresh or dried black olives, finely chopped*

- *Fresh or canned hot chiles, finely chopped*

SUN-DRIED TOMATO DOUGH

A bit of garlic, olive oil, basil, and Parmesan cheese is all that's needed to dress this pasta.

1½ cups	unbleached flour	350 ml
½ tsp	salt	½ tsp
2	sun-dried tomatoes, packed in oil	2
1 tsp	oil from sun-dried tomatoes	1 tsp
1	egg	1

Combine flour and salt. Mince tomatoes almost to a paste. Blend tomatoes and oil with egg; then proceed according to directions for Making Fresh Pasta (see pages 19–21).

Makes 1¼ pounds (570 g) pasta.

CARROT DOUGH

Fantastic color and flavor are strong suits of this delicately colored pasta.

6 oz	raw carrots	170 g
1¾ cups	unbleached flour	425 ml
1	egg	1
1	egg beaten with 1 tbl water	1

Peel carrots and cut into 2-inch (5-cm) pieces. Cook in boiling water for 7–8 minutes. Purée carrots in food processor or blender. Combine flour and egg, add carrot purée, and proceed according to directions for Making Fresh Pasta (see pages 19–21).

Makes 1½ pounds (680 g) pasta.

Making Fresh Pasta

Making your own fresh pasta is easier than you think. The secret to successful homemade pasta is to not overwork the dough—it must stay soft and pliable, but not sticky. Dust pasta with cornstarch or flour to prevent sticking. If not cooking it immediately, let the pasta dry. When completely dry, pasta can be stored in sealed containers or plastic bags on a pantry shelf for up to 3 months.

Making Pasta with a Machine

If you make fresh pasta frequently, a machine may be a practical investment. The following information presents general guidelines for using different kinds of machines. *Be sure to consult the manufacturer's instructions for the specific equipment you are using.*

Heavy-duty kitchen mixer
Attach a flat beater to the mixer, place all ingredients in the mixer bowl, and mix briefly to blend. Turn off machine and replace flat beater with dough hook. Turn on mixer and knead ingredients for about 2 minutes. Turn off mixer, remove dough from bowl, and complete the kneading by hand unless your mixer is designed to knead heavy doughs. Some mixers have attachments for extruding pasta dough.

Food processor Place dry ingredients for pasta dough in the work bowl fitted with a steel blade. Begin processing. With the machine running, add eggs through the feed tube in a slow, steady stream. Process until mixture begins to pull away from the sides of the work bowl. Turn off machine and complete the kneading by hand unless your food processor is designed to knead heavy dough.

Hand-cranked or electric pasta machine Mix and shape the dough into a smooth ball with a kitchen mixer or food processor or by hand. Set the rollers on the pasta machine at the widest opening and feed a piece of dough through until smooth and elastic, about 8 or 10 times. Each time the dough strip comes out, fold it in half before feeding it back into the machine. If the dough gets sticky, dust it lightly with flour. Adjust the roller to the next setting and pass the dough through, leaving it unfolded. Repeat several times

per setting, narrowing the opening one setting each time, until all the dough has been rolled. Dry the dough about 15 minutes before cutting. To cut, adjust the blades to the desired width, pass each dried strip of dough through the blades, and trim pasta to desired length.

Automatic pasta makers

Most automatic pasta makers operate on a common principle: Ingredients are placed in a mixing chamber and mixed and kneaded by a paddle or dough hook. Then the dough is forced through a die plate that forms it into the desired shape. Most automatic machines come with an assortment of die plates for creating both flat and tubular pasta varieties. Follow the manufacturer's instructions for the specific machine you are using.

MAKING PASTA BY HAND

Machines can be convenient for making pasta, but they aren't essential. With only a bowl, a fork, and a rolling pin, you can turn out professional-quality fresh pasta in 10 minutes.

1. Make a ring of flour blended with salt on clean work surface. Place beaten egg in center of well. Use a fork or your fingertips to incorporate the flour into beaten egg to form a firm dough. On a flour-dusted work surface, knead dough until it is smooth and cohesive (5–8 minutes). Cover with damp cloth. Let rest for 15 minutes.

2. Lightly flour work surface. Start with one third of the dough at a time. Starting from the center and moving to the edge, roll the pasta, using as few strokes as possible. If dough becomes too elastic, cover it for a few minutes with a damp cloth to prevent it from drying out. Roll out about ⅛ to ¹⁄₁₆ inch (.3 to .2 cm) thick.

3. Lightly flour dough and roll into a jelly-roll shape. Cut by hand to desired thickness for flat shapes (such as linguine, fettuccine, or lasagne). Dry 10–15 minutes on a pasta rack before cooking.

Pasta Sauces

If there's a secret to perfectly sauced pasta, it's knowing how to prepare a few basic sauces and use them as building blocks to create scores of different dishes. In the following pages you'll find sauces for pasta that also complement many types of meats, chicken, fish, and vegetables.

Northern Italian Tomato Sauce

If you can't get fresh, vine-ripened tomatoes, use the best available canned variety, preferably imported from Italy.

2 tsp	olive oil	2 tsp
4 tsp	butter	4 tsp
1	carrot, peeled and diced	1
2 ribs	celery, diced	2 ribs
1	onion, diced	1
2 tbl	minced garlic	2 tbl
1 tsp	flour	1 tsp
3 lb	ripe tomatoes, peeled, seeded, and chopped (see page 24)	1.4 kg
	or	
1 can (28 oz)	plum tomatoes, whirled briefly in a blender	1 can (800 g)
1 tbl	tomato paste	1 tbl
pinch	sugar	pinch
1 tsp	dried basil	1 tsp
4 sprigs	fresh parsley	4 sprigs
2 sprigs	fresh oregano	2 sprigs
1	bay leaf	1
to taste	salt and freshly ground black pepper	to taste

1. Heat oil and butter in a large, heavy saucepan over moderate heat. Add carrot, celery, onion, and garlic and stew gently for 10 minutes. Stir in flour and continue cooking 5 minutes.

2. Add remaining ingredients except salt and pepper. Simmer, partly covered, for 1 hour.

3. Remove bay leaf and herb stems. Adjust seasoning to taste with salt and pepper.

Makes 4 cups (900 ml).

FRESH TOMATO AND HERB SAUCE

When hot pasta hits peak-of-season tomatoes and fresh herbs, the result is an explosion of aroma and flavor.

3 lb	fresh, ripe tomatoes, peeled, seeded, and chopped (see below)	1.4 kg
2 tbl	garlic, finely minced	2 tbl
½ cup	olive oil	125 ml
¼ cup	chopped fresh basil	60 ml
2 tbl	minced fresh parsley	2 tbl
½ tsp	hot-pepper flakes	½ tsp
to taste	freshly ground black pepper	to taste
1 tbl	balsamic vinegar	1 tbl
1 tsp	salt	1 tsp

1. Combine all ingredients except salt in a large non-aluminum bowl. Stir to blend well; then let sit at room temperature for 30 minutes.

2. Just before serving, add salt.

Makes slightly over 2 cups (500 ml).

PREPARING FRESH TOMATOES

1. *Use a paring knife to core the tomatoes.*

2. *Turn tomatoes over and make an X-shaped cut in the bottom of each tomato.*

3. *Put the tomatoes in boiling water to cover for 15 seconds. Remove them with a slotted spoon and put them in cold water for a few seconds.*

4. *Remove from the cold water and use a paring knife to pull off the skins.*

5. *Halve the tomatoes horizontally with a chopping knife. Hold over a bowl, cut side down, and squeeze to remove the seeds.*

6. *Chop the tomatoes into small pieces.*

CLASSIC BOLOGNESE SAUCE

Rich Italian sauces like this one from Bologna are especially good with sturdy pasta varieties—like shells or rigatoni—that have hollows or ridges to trap bits of meat and vegetables.

½ cup	olive oil	125 ml
½ cup	unsalted butter	125 ml
1½ cups	diced onion	350 ml
1 cup	diced celery	250 ml
1 cup	peeled and diced carrot	250 ml
2 lb	extra-lean ground beef	900 g
1¾ cups	dry white wine	425 ml
1 cup	milk	250 ml
5 lb	ripe tomatoes, peeled, seeded, and chopped (see opposite page)	2.3 kg
	or	
2 cans (28 oz each)	plum tomatoes, whirled briefly in a blender	2 cans (800 g each)
1 tsp	salt	1 tsp
⅛ tsp	freshly grated nutmeg	⅛ tsp
1 tsp	freshly ground black pepper	1 tsp

1. Heat oil and butter in a medium stockpot over moderate heat. When butter foams, add onions, celery, and carrots and cook for 10 minutes.

2. Add beef, breaking it up with a wooden spoon; cook until meat is lightly browned. Add wine and simmer until wine has been completely absorbed. Add milk and simmer until milk has been completely absorbed.

3. Add remaining ingredients and simmer gently, uncovered, until mixture is reduced to a rich sauce (about 2½ hours).

4. Taste and adjust seasoning.

Makes about 4 cups (900 ml).

White Clam or Mussel Sauce

Select the smallest clams available. Fresh mussels are even more flavorful than clams and make a fancy presentation when arranged atop linguine, the classic pasta for this sauce.

2 lb	fresh clams or mussels	900 g
	or	
2 cans (6½ oz each)	chopped clams and their juice	2 cans (185 g each)
¼ cup	olive oil	60 ml
2 cloves	garlic	2 cloves
⅓ cup	dry white wine	85 ml
to taste	freshly ground black pepper	to taste
2 tbl	chopped parsley, for garnish	2 tbl

1. If using canned clams, begin with step 2. If using fresh clams, scrub thoroughly with a stiff brush to remove any specks of sand or barnacles. Place clams in a metal colander and set in a large pot containing approximately 2 inches (5 cm) boiling water. Cover tightly and steam just until shells begin to open. Remove from heat and remove meat from shells. Dice meat and set aside. Strain juice from pan through a paper coffee filter or fine sieve; reserve ½ cup (125 ml) liquid to use for sauce.

2. In a large skillet heat 3 tablespoons of the olive oil over medium heat. Add garlic cloves and brown lightly to flavor the oil; then discard garlic.

3. Add steamed fresh clams or canned clams along with their juice and white wine. Cook over medium-high heat until about half of the liquid has evaporated (about 2 minutes). Add pepper to taste and simmer 4–5 minutes.

4. Garnish with parsley.

Makes about 1½ cups (350 ml).

CHÈVRE AND WALNUT SAUCE

Serve this sauce with plain or spinach fettuccine.

2 cups	half-and-half	500 ml
8 oz	chèvre (goat's milk cheese)	225 g
2 cloves	garlic, minced	2 cloves
¾ cup	coarsely chopped toasted walnuts	175 ml
⅓ cup	finely chopped parsley	85 ml
to taste	salt and freshly ground black pepper	to taste

1. In a medium saucepan combine half-and-half, chèvre, and garlic. Heat, stirring until mixture is creamy and smooth. Bring to a boil.

2. Boil gently about 10 minutes to thicken sauce and reduce it to about 2¼ cups (550 ml). Stir occasionally at first, then frequently the last few minutes to prevent scorching.

3. Remove from heat; stir in walnuts and parsley. Season to taste with salt and pepper. Use immediately or cool to room temperature and refrigerate or freeze.

Makes 2¼ cups (550 ml).

MATCHING PASTA WITH SAUCES

Here are some classic combinations:

Meat sauces Bowties, cannelloni, fusilli, lasagne, linguine, macaroni, rigatoni, rotelle, shells, ziti

Shellfish sauces Fettuccine, linguine, spaghetti, vermicelli

Cheese and creamy sauces Fettuccine, lasagne, linguine, macaroni, tortellini

Mushroom sauces Fettuccine, fusilli, linguine, rotelle, ziti

Tomato sauces Bowties, lasagne, penne, spaghetti

Pesto or oil sauces Angel hair, fusilli, linguine, spaghetti, tortellini

CURRIED CREAM SAUCE

Serve with spinach linguine (see photo on opposite page).

2 tbl	butter	2 tbl
2 tbl	flour	2 tbl
2 cups	half-and-half	500 ml
½–1 tsp	curry powder	½–1 tsp
½–1 lb	tiny shrimp, cooked	225–450 g
½–¾ cup	freshly grated Parmesan cheese	125–175 ml

1. In a medium saucepan melt butter. Add flour and cook, stirring, until bubbly. Blend in half-and-half and curry powder. Bring to a boil and cook until slightly thickened.

2. Fold in shrimp and Parmesan cheese.

Makes about 2½ cups (600 ml).

SAUCE AMANDINE

Sprinkle with minced parsley and black pepper for extra zip.

⅔ cup	ground dry-roasted almonds	150 ml
6–8 oz	prosciutto, diced (optional)	170–225 g
½ cup	shredded provolone cheese	125 ml
2–3 tbl	half-and-half	2–3 tbl
1	egg	1
1 clove	garlic, minced	1 clove
½ tsp	Italian herb seasoning	½ tsp
as needed	chopped almonds, for garnish	as needed

1. Mix together almonds, prosciutto, provolone, half-and-half beaten with egg, garlic, and herb seasoning.

2. Garnish with chopped almonds.

Makes about 2¼ cups (550 ml).

Melanzane Sauce

This sauce tastes best when made ahead. Serve it with spaghetti.

1½ tbl	olive oil	1½ tbl
1	onion, chopped	1
3 cloves	garlic, minced	3 cloves
1 can (28 oz)	tomatoes, undrained	1 can (800 g)
¼ cup	dry red or white wine	60 ml
1–1½ lb	eggplant, unpeeled and cut in ¾-inch (1.9-cm) cubes	450–680 g
2 cups (¼ lb)	sliced mushrooms	500 ml (115 g)
¾ tsp each	dried basil and oregano	¾ tsp each
½ tsp	sugar	½ tsp
to taste	salt and freshly ground black pepper	to taste

1. In a wide-bottomed pan or skillet with high sides over medium-high heat, heat oil. Add onion and garlic; sauté about 2 minutes.

2. Break tomatoes into bits. Add to pan with their juice, wine, eggplant, mushrooms, herbs, and sugar.

3. Cover pan and simmer 5 minutes. Remove cover and cook over medium heat until sauce reduces and thickens, 10–15 minutes.

4. Season to taste with salt and pepper. Cool to room temperature and serve at once or refrigerate or freeze until ready to use.

Makes 5 to 6 cups (1.1–1.4 l).

Preparing Eggplant

Choose eggplants that feel heavy for their size, with smooth, shiny skin and firm flesh.

Wash and trim the stem ends; do not peel. If you are using a large globe variety, slice and liberally salt the flesh to remove excess moisture; then press for one hour between towels weighted with a heavy plate. Rinse and pat dry before cooking.

Parmigiano Cream Sauce

Use this delicate northern Italian sauce to dress up almost any pasta.

2 tbl	olive oil	2 tbl
1 tbl	butter	1 tbl
3 tbl	minced shallots	3 tbl
½ cup	heavy cream	125 ml
½ cup	freshly grated Parmesan cheese	125 ml

1. Heat olive oil and butter in a skillet over moderate heat. Add shallots; cook gently until soft.

2. Add cream; cook over low heat 3–4 minutes more, whisking to incorporate cream. Stir in Parmesan cheese.

Makes about 1 cup (250 ml).

Mushroom Sauce

Try this with porcini mushrooms (see page 49).

2 tbl	olive oil	2 tbl
1 lb	mushrooms, coarsely chopped	450 g
⅓ cup	chopped green onion	85 ml
1–2 cloves	garlic, minced	1–2 cloves
½ cup	white wine or chicken broth	125 ml
1	bay leaf	1
½ tsp	Worcestershire sauce	½ tsp
½ tsp each	dried basil and dried oregano	½ tsp each
½ tsp	salt	½ tsp
to taste	freshly grated Parmesan cheese	to taste

1. In a large frying pan, heat oil. Add mushrooms, green onion, and garlic; sauté briefly.

2. Stir in remaining ingredients except cheese. Simmer 10–15 minutes. Top with freshly grated Parmesan cheese.

Makes about 2 cups (500 ml).

Quattro Formaggi Sauce

A quartet of famous cheeses adds unusual flavor and texture to this sauce.

1 cup each	Gruyère and fontina cheese, finely cubed	250 ml each
2 cups	freshly grated Romano cheese	500 ml
2 tbl	flour	2 tbl
¼ cup	butter	60 ml
1 cup	half-and-half or evaporated skim milk	250 ml
1 tsp	dried basil, rosemary, or thyme	1 tsp
½–¾ cup	freshly grated Parmesan cheese	125–175 ml

1. Toss Gruyère, fontina, and Romano cheeses with flour. In a heavy-bottomed saucepan, heat butter and half-and-half until butter melts.

2. Gradually stir in cheeses and cook over medium heat until sauce is smooth.

3. Add basil, rosemary, or thyme. Just before serving, toss with Parmesan cheese.

Makes about 4½ cups (1 l).

Cooking with Cheese

Cheese adds distinctive flavor to countless sauces, but it needs careful handling. Sauces containing cheese should not be heated too long or at too high a temperature. Prolonged cooking causes the casein in cheese to coagulate and separate from the fat and water, producing a stringy, oily sauce. Add grated or cubed cheese slowly to a sauce over low or moderate heat, stirring constantly to blend. Once cheese has melted, remove sauce from heat or keep warm over hot (not boiling) water until ready to use.

PESTO SAUCE

No doubt everyone who loves basil has a favorite way to make pesto: Some cooks use walnuts or hazelnuts instead of pine nuts, or sun-dried tomatoes instead of either nuts or butter. In place of sweet basil, the most commonly grown variety, some cooks prefer lemon, opal, purple ruffled, Thai, or Greek basil, which produce exciting variations in the flavor and color of pesto made with them. Whatever ingredients you use, the aroma and taste of pesto is unforgettable, whether it's tossed with hot linguine or stirred into steaming soup.

2 cups	fresh basil leaves, loosely packed	500 ml
½ cup	extra virgin olive oil	125 ml
2 tbl	pine nuts, toasted	2 tbl
4 cloves	garlic, minced	4 cloves
1 tsp	salt	1 tsp
½ cup	freshly grated Parmesan cheese	125 ml
2 tbl	freshly grated Romano cheese	2 tbl
3 tbl	unsalted butter, softened	3 tbl

1. Put basil, olive oil, pine nuts, garlic, and salt in a blender or food processor. Blend or process until smooth.

2. Transfer to a bowl and stir in remaining ingredients.

Makes 1 cup (250 ml).

PRESERVING PESTO

Pesto is traditionally a sauce for summer, best made when basil is abundant and inexpensive. You can make it up to 1 week ahead, cover it with a film of olive oil, and refrigerate it in an airtight container. If you plan to freeze it, make the pesto without the garlic, Parmesan cheese, or butter; add these items just before serving the thawed pesto. You can freeze pesto for up to 1 month, covered with a film of olive oil. Or freeze pesto in ice-cube trays, unmold, and store the cubes in a lock-top plastic bag. Use 3–6 cubes per serving of pasta.

Italian Sausage and Pepper Sauce

"Hot" Italian sausage varieties are laced with hot red pepper; "sweet"
varieties usually have fennel seed in place of the pepper. For a lowfat
sauce, substitute chicken or turkey sausage. Serve over rigatoni or ziti.

½ lb each	hot and sweet Italian pork sausages (casings removed)	225 g each
	or	
1 lb	bulk sausage	450 g
1	green pepper, seeded and cut in strips	1
¼ cup	sliced red onion	60 ml
1 clove	garlic, minced	1 clove
1 tsp	dried oregano	1 tsp
½ tsp each	dried basil, thyme, and salt	½ tsp each
¼ tsp	freshly ground black pepper	¼ tsp
1 can (28 oz)	plum tomatoes	1 can (800 g)
as needed	Parmesan cheese, grated	as needed

1. In a large frying pan, sauté sausage until browned. Drain all but 1 tablespoon fat. Add green pepper, red onion, garlic, oregano, basil, thyme, salt, and pepper. Sauté until pepper and onion are tender (10 minutes), stirring frequently.

2. Stir in plum tomatoes (and liquid), breaking up with a fork. Simmer to reduce liquid and heat ingredients through (about 5 minutes). Top with grated Parmesan cheese to taste.

Makes about 6 cups (1.4 l).

PASTA SOUPS AND SALADS

Pasta soups and salads make perfect mealtime openers or a satisfying light meal. Keep them in mind the next time you're packing a lunch for yourself or someone special. Like many other dishes based on pasta, soups and salads offer creative, delicious opportunities for using up leftover shellfish, poultry, meats, or vegetables.

MINESTRONE VERDURA

Minestrone in Italian refers to all hearty soups. Try a topping of Pesto Sauce (see page 33) on this classic main-course soup. Use the larger amount of fusilli if you like your minestrone thick.

2	carrots	2
½ lb	green beans	225 g
2	zucchini	2
1 can (28 oz)	whole tomatoes	1 can (800 g)
1 tbl	olive oil	1 tbl
1	onion, diced	1
2 stalks	celery, diced	2 stalks
4 cloves	garlic, minced	4 cloves
½ cup	parsley, minced	125 ml
3 tbl	fresh basil, minced	3 tbl
3 tbl	fresh oregano, minced	3 tbl
2	bay leaves	2
4 tsp	salt	4 tsp
1 tsp	freshly ground black pepper	1 tsp
3 cups	cooked, small white beans	700 ml
⅓–½ lb	fusilli	100–225 g
½ cup	grated Parmesan cheese, for garnish	125 ml

1. Peel carrots and cut into ½-inch (1.25-cm) sections. Trim stem ends from green beans and cut into ½-inch (1.25-cm) lengths. Cut zucchini into ½-inch (1.25-cm) cubes. Core tomatoes and cut into ½-inch (1.25-cm) cubes.

2. Heat oil in an 8-quart (7.2-l) stockpot or Dutch oven over low heat. Cook onion, celery, and garlic for 6 minutes. Add carrots, tomatoes, parsley, basil, oregano, bay leaves, 12 cups (2.7 l) water, salt, pepper, white beans, and pasta. Bring to a boil, reduce heat to medium, and simmer for 20 minutes. Add green beans and cook for 5 minutes. Add zucchini and cook for 3 minutes more. Ladle into individual shallow soup plates and sprinkle with Parmesan cheese.

Makes 14 cups (3.2 l), 8 to 12 servings.

Pasta e Fagioli

If you make this soup a day ahead, wait to add the pasta until just before you serve it. Look for the pancetta, a type of unsmoked bacon, in Italian markets.

2 cups	dried Great Northern white beans or cannellini beans	500 ml
¼ cup	olive oil	60 ml
2 oz	pancetta, diced	60 g
1 cup	chopped onion	250 ml
½ cup	diced celery	125 ml
½ cup	diced carrot	125 ml
1½ tbl	sliced garlic	1½ tbl
4½ cups	tomatoes, peeled, seeded, and diced (see page 24)	1 l
to taste	salt and freshly ground black pepper	to taste
5 oz	shells or bowties	140 g
to taste	freshly grated Parmesan cheese	to taste
to taste	extra virgin olive oil	to taste

1. Soak beans overnight in water to cover (no need to refrigerate). The next day heat the ¼ cup (60 ml) olive oil in a large stockpot over moderate heat. Add pancetta and render slightly (about 3 minutes). Add onion and sauté until soft and translucent (about 3 minutes). Add celery, carrot, and garlic and sauté gently another 5 minutes, stirring occasionally.

2. Drain beans and add to pot along with 9 cups (2 l) fresh water and tomatoes. Cover and simmer 1½ hours, or until beans are tender. Season to taste with salt and pepper.

3. Cook pasta until tender in boiling salted water; drain well, add to soup, and heat through. Cool soup slightly before serving. Serve it in warm bowls, topped with a sprinkle of Parmesan cheese and a drizzle of extra virgin olive oil.

Makes 12 to 14 cups (2.7–3.2 l), about 12 servings.

Pasta Soup Basics

The tantalizing texture of pasta plus the comforting warmth of soup—the best of both worlds is yours with pasta soup. The right pasta transforms simple soup into something sensational.

Pasta Varieties for Soup

The best varieties of pasta for soup are those that cook relatively quickly and that are easy to eat with a spoon:

Pastina Small decorative shapes designed for cooking in broth or soup include acini de pepe ("peppercorns"), ditali ("thimbles"), ruote ("wheels"), semi di melone ("melon seeds"), and tubettini ("little tubes").

Small filled varieties Raviolini, tortellini, and other petite pastas with fillings can turn soup into a main course.

Other varieties Angel hair and vermicelli pasta add body and flavor to broths or thin soups. (Breaking long pasta into pieces before cooking makes it easier to eat with a spoon.) Macaroni, rotelle, or shells go well in hearty soups. Gnocchi simmered in rich broth makes an especially satisfying soup. Tiny alphabet letters, stars, and animals are among the most popular novelty varieties for soup.

Cooking Pasta for Soup

Pastina and fine long pasta such as angel hair or vermicelli can be cooked directly in simmering broth or soup, without precooking.

Dense shapes such as rotelle or bowties usually need precooking in boiling salted water before adding them to soup.

If you plan to prepare soup ahead and refrigerate or freeze it, wait to add the pasta until you reheat the soup. Otherwise, the pasta may absorb too much liquid, resulting in a heavy pudding-textured soup.

"Straw and Hay" in Broth

Yellow egg pasta and green spinach noodles resemble "straw and hay" afloat in a rich meat stock. This classic soup makes an elegant introduction to a main course. For a casual meal, serve the soup as the main event with Italian or French bread.

1 qt	beef or chicken stock	900 ml
3½ oz	fresh spinach fettuccine	100 g
	(use Spinach Dough, page 16),	
	in 6-inch (15-cm) lengths	
3½ oz	fresh egg fettuccine	100 g
	(use Basic Egg Dough, page 15),	
	in 6-inch (15-cm) lengths	
to taste	salt	to taste
¼ cup	freshly grated Parmesan cheese	60 ml

1. Bring stock to a simmer in a large stockpot. In a separate pot, bring a large amount of salted water to a boil. Add both spinach and egg fettuccine and cook until just wilted (about 20–25 seconds). Drain, transfer to the simmering stock, and simmer until pasta is al dente. Season broth to taste with salt.

2. Ladle soup into warm serving bowls and top each serving with grated Parmesan cheese.

Makes about 7 cups (1.6 l), 4 to 6 servings.

MAKING TORTELLINI

Tortellini can be made with a variety of fillings, including the pumpkin filling shown here (see recipe on opposite page). Tortellini can be formed a few hours ahead and spread on lightly floured baking sheets. Make sure they do not touch. Cover and refrigerate or freeze before cooking. Follow directions for freezing ravioli (see page 84).

2. Fold circle in half to enclose filling; press edges firmly to seal.

1. The dough should be quite thin. Cut 2-inch (5-cm) circles from dough. Put a scant teaspoon of filling in center of each. Brush edges lightly with cold water.

3. With sealed edge out, place folded circle over index finger. Bring ends toward each other under the finger, turning sealed outer edge up to form a cuff. Pinch ends together firmly. Let dry for a few minutes on a lightly floured surface before cooking.

Pumpkin Tortellini Soup

Delicious in broth or tossed with butter or olive oil, these pumpkin-flavored tortellini also make a fine accompaniment to the holiday turkey.

Pumpkin Filling

½ cup	cooked, puréed pumpkin or winter squash	125 ml
⅔ cup	freshly grated Parmesan cheese	150 g
¼ cup	ricotta cheese	60 ml
2	eggs	2
1	egg yolk	1
1 tbl	brandy	1 tbl
1 tsp	powdered sage	1 tsp
to taste	salt and freshly ground black pepper	to taste
pinch	nutmeg	pinch
2 recipes	Basic Egg Dough	2 recipes
	or other pasta dough (see pages 15–18)	
	or 1 recipe each of two different kinds	
6 cups	chicken stock	1.4 l

1. To prepare filling, combine pumpkin, Parmesan cheese, ricotta, eggs, egg yolk, brandy, and sage in a bowl. Season to taste with salt, pepper, and nutmeg.

2. Roll out pasta and form tortellini as shown on opposite page, using a teaspoon of filling for each one. You will have 36–40 tortellini. Bring stock to a boil in a saucepan. Add tortellini. They will sink, then float. After they float to the surface, cook 2 minutes. Remove one and taste for doneness. Transfer cooked tortellini to warm soup plates. Ladle 1 cup hot chicken stock over each portion.

Serves 6.

FETA SALAD WITH ROTELLE

This variation on a traditional Greek salad combines rotelle with a light vinaigrette.

4 cups	rotelle	900 ml
1 cup	crumbled feta cheese	250 ml
¼ cup	olive oil	60 ml
1 cup	peeled and sliced cucumber	250 ml
2	tomatoes, peeled, seeded, and sliced into strips (see page 24)	2
¼ cup	pitted Greek olives	60 ml
1 tbl	dried oregano	1 tbl
to taste	salt and freshly ground black pepper	to taste

1. Cook and drain pasta. Combine with remaining ingredients.

2. Let chill for 30 minutes before serving.

Serves 6.

STOCKING A PASTA PANTRY

Even the most organized and conscientious cooks have days when the refrigerator seems almost empty. At times like those, you'll appreciate being able to reach into the pantry and quickly pull together a tasty, satisfying dish like the one on the opposite page or Pasta Puttanesca (see page 55). It's easy to do if you keep the following ingredients on hand:

dried pasta (see page 10)
olive oil (see page 58)
canned tomatoes
bottled capers
bottled olives
canned beans (kidney, cannellini, garbanzo)
bottled artichokes

dried herbs
dried mushrooms (see page 49)
sun-dried tomatoes
garlic
onions
shallots
peppercorns
red pepper flakes

Pantry Pasta Salad

You can easily vary the ingredients in this dish. Try it with garbanzo or navy beans instead of kidney beans, rotelle or shells instead of fusilli, and a tablespoon of pickled capers instead of the artichokes.

½ cup	dried mushrooms	125 ml
1 can (28 oz)	whole plum tomatoes	1 can (800 g)
1 tbl	olive oil	1 tbl
1	onion, diced	1
2 cloves	garlic, minced	2 cloves
1 tsp	salt	1 tsp
1 tsp	dried basil	1 tsp
1 tsp	dried oregano	1 tsp
1 tsp	dried parsley	1 tsp
¼ tsp	ground chiles	¼ tsp
1 can (5¾ oz)	black olives, quartered	1 can (165 g)
1 can (15¼ oz)	kidney beans	1 can (435 g)
1 can (14 oz)	artichokes, quartered	1 can (400 g)
1 lb	fusilli	450 g

1. Soak mushrooms in ½ cup (125 ml) hot water for 30 minutes. Drain tomatoes and reserve juice. Chop each tomato into 6 pieces.

2. Heat oil in a 3-quart (2.7-l) saucepan. Sauté onion until translucent (5–7 minutes). Add garlic and cook 5 minutes more. Drain mushrooms and cut into thin slices. Add mushrooms, tomatoes, salt, basil, oregano, parsley, chiles, and reserved tomato juice. Simmer for 10 minutes. Add olives, kidney beans, and artichokes. Simmer for 15 minutes.

3. Cook and drain pasta. Place in a shallow serving bowl. Add sauce and toss to combine. Serve at room temperature.

Serves 6 to 8.

CURRIED PRAWN AND PASTA SALAD

Cooked prawns tossed with rotelle and a curried mayonnaise dressing, garnished with chopped, toasted almonds make a fine lunch or supper dish. This seafood salad keeps well for three days and is best served chilled on a bed of lettuce leaves or spinach.

2 cups	rotelle	500 ml
1 lb	medium prawns, peeled and deveined	450 g
⅔ cup	white wine	150 ml
¼ tsp	freshly ground black pepper	¼ tsp
½ cup	minced celery	125 ml
½ cup	mayonnaise	125 ml
1 tsp	lemon juice	1 tsp
2 tsp	curry powder	2 tsp
as needed	lettuce leaves, for lining platter or salad plates	as needed
1 tbl	chopped, toasted almonds	1 tbl

1. Cook and drain pasta. Set aside.

2. In a small saucepan over medium-high heat, cook prawns in wine until prawns turn pink (about 2 minutes). Remove prawns and cut in half. Discard wine.

2. In a large bowl mix pasta with cooked prawns, pepper, celery, mayonnaise, lemon juice, and curry powder. Chill 20 minutes. Arrange on a bed of lettuce and garnish with almonds.

Serves 4.

Basil and Bowtie Salad

Bowties are a good medium for vividly flavored basil-and-garlic dressing. This salad would be a welcome addition to a brown bag lunch. You might also serve it as a supper side dish with sautéed shrimp or with roast chicken.

3 cups	bowties	700 ml
3 tbl	red wine vinegar	3 tbl
½ cup	fresh basil leaves, loosely packed	125 ml
2 cloves	garlic, minced or pressed	2 cloves
½ tsp	salt	½ tsp
¼ tsp	sugar	¼ tsp
⅓ cup	grated Parmesan cheese	85 ml
½ cup	olive oil	125 ml
to taste	freshly ground black pepper	to taste
as needed	cherry tomatoes, for garnish	as needed

1. Cook and drain pasta. Set aside.

2. In blender or food processor combine vinegar, basil, garlic, salt, sugar, cheese, and olive oil. Whirl or process until smooth and well combined.

3. Lightly mix pasta and dressing. Cover and refrigerate for 1 hour or longer to blend flavors. Sprinkle with pepper and garnish with cherry tomatoes before serving.

Serves 4 to 6.

Marinated Mushroom Pasta Salad

Here's a simple way to bypass the costly, high-calorie marinated mushrooms sold at the store. The marinade has a hint of burgundy wine.

8 oz	vermicelli, broken into 6-inch (15-cm) lengths	225 g
2 cups	halved button mushrooms	500 ml
½ cup	trimmed snow peas	125 ml
½ cup	seeded and julienned red bell pepper	125 ml
2 tbl	drained capers	2 tbl
2 tsp	olive oil	2 tsp
2 tbl	red wine vinegar	2 tbl
1 tbl	lemon juice	1 tbl
1 tbl	salt	1 tbl
1 tbl	burgundy wine	1 tbl
2 tsp	honey	2 tsp
dash	freshly ground black pepper	dash
1 tsp	dill	1 tsp

1. Cook and drain pasta. Set aside.

2. In a large salad bowl, combine mushrooms, snow peas, bell pepper, capers, and pasta. Toss well.

3. In another bowl mix remaining ingredients. Taste for seasoning. Pour over pasta mixture and mix well. Chill before serving.

Serves 4.

Marvelous Mushrooms

The common button mushroom (agaricus bisporum) is mild-tasting and perennially available. Other mushrooms for pasta include the cultivated or wild oyster mushroom, a mild-flavored variety available year-round; porcini, among the most highly prized wild mushroom (available fresh, dried, or canned); and chanterelle (available fresh, dried, or canned), a highly flavorful wild variety with a hearty texture.

CHINESE PASTA SALAD

This light Asian-accented pasta salad is a cinch to make, and it will keep, well covered, for about two days in the refrigerator. If you decide to store it longer than two to three hours, wait and add the snow peas right before serving, as they tend to discolor quickly. If you like your salads spicy, add more cayenne pepper.

3 cups	rotelle	700 ml
1 cup	trimmed, whole snow peas	250 ml
2	red bell peppers, seeded and julienned	2
1 tsp	sesame seed	1 tsp
½ tsp	cayenne pepper	½ tsp
¼ cup	tamari or soy sauce	60 ml
3 tbl	Asian sesame oil	3 tbl
3 tbl	lemon juice	3 tbl
2 tbl	grated onion	2 tbl
2 tbl	minced garlic	2 tbl
pinch	dried dill	pinch
dash	freshly ground black pepper	dash
as needed	lettuce leaves, for lining bowl	as needed

1. Cook and drain pasta.

2. Combine all ingredients except lettuce leaves. Let chill for 30 minutes.

3. Serve on lettuce leaves in a bowl.

Serves 4.

Tortellini Salad with Thai Dressing

Crisp, cool vegetables and soft tortellini make a refreshing alternative to a heavy meal on a warm summer day.

24 oz	fresh or frozen tortellini	680 g

Thai Dressing

4–6 tbl	rice vinegar	4–6 tbl
3–3½ tbl	soy sauce	3–3½ tbl
1 clove	garlic, minced	1 clove
2 tbl	minced fresh ginger	2 tbl
1½ tsp	sugar	1½ tsp
¾ tsp	hot-pepper flakes	¾ tsp
¾ tsp	dry mustard	¾ tsp
¼ tsp	five-spice powder	¼ tsp
¼ cup	sesame oil	60 ml
½	red bell pepper, finely diced	½
⅓ cup	chopped green onions	85 ml
⅔ cup	snow peas, cut diagonally	150 ml
1	carrot, cut into 2-inch (5-cm) strips	1
as needed	Chinese (napa) cabbage or spinach leaves, for lining platter or salad plates	as needed

1. Cook and drain tortellini according to package directions. Place in a large bowl.

2. To make dressing, combine 4 tablespoons vinegar, 3 table-spoons soy sauce, garlic, ginger, sugar, hot-pepper flakes, dry mustard, and five-spice powder in a small bowl. Whisk in oil.

3. Toss warm tortellini with dressing. Toss in red bell pepper, green onion, snow peas, and carrot. Add more vinegar and soy sauce to taste, if desired.

4. Line a serving platter or individual serving plates with cabbage or spinach leaves. Arrange salad over greens. Serve at room temperature.

Serves 4 to 6.

QUICK AND EASY PASTA ENTRÉES

When you want great food in a hurry, pasta is the answer. The following pages present an assortment of uncomplicated but appealing pasta entrées for lunches, light meals, and suppers. From speedy classics to clever but quick new interpretations of traditional dishes, the selection of fast pasta fare you'll find here offers the busiest cook plenty to choose from.

PASTA PUTTANESCA

Pasta Puttanesca is a dish of delicious simplicity and convenience. According to legend, ancient Rome's "ladies of the night" favored this recipe because of its quick preparation, thus earning it the title of "harlot's pasta." It can be made almost entirely from ingredients on hand in your pantry (see Stocking a Pasta Pantry on page 44).

2	onions, diced	2
4 tbl	olive oil	4 tbl
4 cloves	garlic, minced	4 cloves
1 can (28 oz)	whole plum tomatoes, drained and diced	1 can (800 g)
24	black olives, pitted and halved	24
1 tsp	hot-pepper flakes	1 tsp
1 tsp	dried oregano	1 tsp
1 tsp	dried basil	1 tsp
1 tsp	salt	1 tsp
¼ tsp	freshly ground black pepper	¼ tsp
4 cups	fusilli or other dried pasta	900 ml
½ cup	grated Asiago or Parmesan cheese, for garnish	125 ml

1. In a medium saucepan or large skillet over medium heat, sauté onions in oil until translucent (about 4 minutes). Add garlic and cook 3 minutes. Stir in tomatoes, olives, hot-pepper flakes, oregano, basil, salt, and pepper; reduce heat to medium-low and simmer 15 minutes. Set aside and keep warm.

2. Cook and drain pasta. Toss with sauce and serve immediately, sprinkled with Asiago or Parmesan cheese.

Serves 6.

FETTUCCINE CARBONARA

In this classic dish, the heat of the pasta cooks the eggs, creating a thick sauce right in the serving bowl. If you can't find pancetta, a type of unsmoked bacon available in Italian markets, substitute bacon.

1 recipe	Basic Egg Dough (see page 15)	1 recipe
2 tbl	olive oil	2 tbl
1 tbl	unsalted butter	1 tbl
2 tbl	finely minced garlic	2 tbl
8 oz	pancetta, in small dice	225 g
⅓ cup	dry white wine	85 ml
2	eggs	2
⅓ cup	freshly grated Romano cheese	85 ml
⅓ cup	freshly grated Parmesan cheese	85 ml
to taste	salt and freshly ground black pepper	to taste

1. Prepare Basic Egg Dough. Roll out and cut dough into fettuccine. Set aside.

2. Heat oil and butter in a skillet over moderate heat. When butter foams, add garlic and sauté until garlic is fragrant. Add pancetta and fry until it is lightly browned. Add wine and simmer until wine is almost completely evaporated. Remove skillet from heat.

3. Break eggs into a large serving bowl and beat lightly. Stir in Romano and Parmesan cheese.

4. Cook and drain pasta. Add to egg-cheese mixture and toss well; then add hot pancetta mixture and toss again. Season with salt and plenty of pepper.

Serves 4.

Fresh Fettuccine Alfredo

One of the quickest pasta dishes to prepare if you have fresh homemade or purchased fettuccine on hand, this simple classic also lends itself to additions of cooked ham or chicken, fresh or canned clams, herbs, or vegetables. This recipe is particularly efficient: The fresh pasta and sauce cook in the same pan and at the same time.

2 tbl	butter	2 tbl
1 tbl	olive oil	1 tbl
3	shallots, minced	3
3 cups	milk	700 ml
12 oz	fresh fettuccine	350 g
1¼ cups	freshly grated Parmesan cheese	300 ml
¼ tsp	white pepper	¼ tsp
1 tbl	chopped parsley, for garnish	1 tbl

1. In a heavy saucepan over medium heat, melt butter with olive oil. Sauté shallots until softened, but not browned (about 5 minutes). Add milk, increase heat to medium-high, and bring to a boil.

2. Stir in fresh fettuccine, reduce heat to medium-low, and simmer, stirring constantly, until pasta is tender (3–4 minutes). Toss with 1 cup (250 ml) of the Parmesan cheese and season with pepper. Serve immediately, sprinkled with additional Parmesan cheese and parsley.

Serves 4.

Fettuccine Fits In Anywhere

Richly sauced fettuccine dishes such as the one above and Fettuccine Carbonara (see opposite page) are satisfying enough to be served as a main course, or, in smaller portions, as a luncheon entrée. But these versatile pasta ribbons also figure in elsewhere on the menu: in broth or soup (see page 40); as a side dish with chicken, veal, or fish; and even as a dessert (see page 91).

Spaghetti with Garlic and Olive Oil

The flavor of a straightforward sauce like this one depends on the quality of the olive oil (see below). Choose young, fresh garlic.

1 head	young garlic	1 head
½ cup	virgin olive oil	125 ml
1 tbl	unsalted butter	1 tbl
1 lb	dried spaghetti	450 g
pinch	hot-pepper flakes	pinch
2 tbl	minced anchovies	2 tbl
to taste	salt and freshly ground black pepper	to taste

1. Separate garlic into cloves. Peel and chop cloves. Heat oil and butter in a skillet over moderate heat. Add garlic and sauté until fragrant. Remove from heat and let stand 20 minutes.

2. Cook and drain pasta. Transfer to a warm serving bowl. Reheat garlic and oil mixture, stirring in pepper flakes and anchovies. Add sauce to pasta and toss well. Season to taste with salt and pepper. Serve immediately.

Serves 4.

The Best Oils for Pasta

The subtle flavor of pasta is enhanced by good-quality olive oil. The flavor and quality of olive oil varies according to the type of olives it was pressed from, where the olives were grown, and the method of pressing. Olive oils are graded according to how much oleic acid they contain and the procedure used to make them. The oil must have been pressed from olives that were not chemically treated in order to qualify for one of the following top four categories:

- *virgin (no more than 4 percent oleic acid)*

- *superfine virgin (no more than 2 percent)*

- *fine virgin (no more than 3 percent)*

- *extra virgin (no more than 1 percent)*

EGGPLANT AND YELLOW PEPPER VERMICELLI

The flavor of this dish comes from the fresh basil, olive oil, Greek olives, and capers.

¼ cup	olive oil	60 ml
¼–½ cup	white wine	60–125 ml
2 cloves	garlic, minced	2 cloves
2 cups	chopped tomato	500 ml
2	Japanese-style eggplants, peeled and cubed	2
2	sweet yellow bell peppers	2
2 tbl	pitted Greek olives	2 tbl
2 tbl	capers	2 tbl
2 tbl	chopped fresh basil	2 tbl
1 lb	vermicelli	450 g
3 tbl	grated Parmesan cheese	3 tbl
to taste	freshly ground black pepper	to taste

1. In a skillet heat olive oil and ¼ cup (60 ml) wine and sauté garlic for 1 minute at medium-high heat. Add tomato and eggplant and continue to cook, stirring frequently, for 10 minutes more, adding wine if the mixture seems dry.

2. Preheat broiler. Cut bell peppers in half and seed them. Place cut side down on an aluminum-foil-lined baking sheet and broil until skins turn black (about 5 minutes). Place blackened peppers into a paper bag and seal top. Let peppers sweat in the bag for 10 minutes; then remove and rinse under cold water, rubbing off the blackened skin with your fingers. Chop the peeled peppers coarsely and add to the sautéed mixture.

3. Add olives, capers, and basil to sauté. Toss with sautéed mixture.

4. Cook and drain pasta. Place in warm serving bowl. Sprinkle with Parmesan cheese and black pepper. Serve immediately.

Serves 6.

Spinach-Ricotta Stuffed Shells

These giant stuffed shells are easy to assemble and they freeze well, so prepare a double recipe and freeze a portion to serve another time.

½ recipe	Northern Italian Tomato Sauce (see page 22)	½ recipe
12 oz	jumbo shells (about 20)	350 g
9 oz	frozen creamed spinach	255 g
1 cup	ricotta cheese	250 ml
1 cup	grated mozzarella cheese	250 ml
½ tsp	salt	½ tsp
¼ tsp	freshly ground black pepper	¼ tsp
¾ cup	chopped walnuts	175 ml

1. Prepare sauce. Set aside and keep warm.

2. Cook and drain shells according to package directions. Set aside.

3. Cook spinach according to package directions and place in bowl. Let cool slightly. Stir in cheeses, salt, and pepper. Stuff each shell with 1 tablespoon spinach mixture. Arrange stuffed shells in a 2-quart (1.8-l) baking dish and set aside.

4. Preheat oven to 350°F (175°C). In a saucepan combine walnuts and sauce and heat until sauce bubbles.

5. Pour heated sauce over stuffed shells. Cover baking dish with foil and bake 30 minutes. Remove foil and bake 10 minutes more. Serve immediately.

Serves 4 to 6.

LINGUINE WITH WINTER PESTO

This easy dish uses parsley and spinach, which are abundant in winter—when basil is scarce.

1 lb	linguine	450 g
½ cup	minced spinach leaves	125 ml
½ cup	chopped parsley	125 ml
1 tbl	dried basil	1 tbl
1 tbl	minced garlic	1 tbl
¼ cup	coarsely chopped walnuts	60 ml
3 tbl	extra virgin olive oil	3 tbl
¼ cup	grated Parmesan cheese	60 ml

1. Cook and drain pasta. Set aside and keep warm.

2. Combine all other ingredients in a blender or food processor, and blend until a thick paste is formed.

3. Toss pasta with pesto. Serve at once.

Serves 4.

STORING AND USING OLIVE OIL

- *Choose olive oil with a clean, fruity aroma, full body, and fruity or peppery flavor.*

- *Store olive oil where it will not be exposed to heat or light, which can cause it to become rancid. Use within a year's time.*

- *Use a good-tasting afford- able olive oil for sautéed and baked dishes; save the finest grades (see The Best Oils for Pasta on page 58) for pesto and other uncooked dishes or for drizzling over cooked foods just before serving.*

Scampi Fettuccine

The fragrance of fresh pasta, garlic, and basil heighten the enjoyment of this dish. Placed on a heated tray, it holds up well at a party buffet. If you substitute dried fettuccine for the fresh, cook the pasta 5 minutes or more.

1 lb	fresh fettuccine	450 g
1 lb	large prawns	450 g
½ cup	white wine	125 ml
2 tsp	olive oil	2 tsp
2 tbl	minced garlic	2 tbl
¼ cup	minced red bell pepper	60 ml
¼ cup	chopped parsley	60 ml

1. Cook and drain pasta. Set aside and keep warm.

2. Peel and devein prawns. In a large skillet over medium-high heat, sauté prawns in wine until they turn bright pink (4–5 minutes). Remove from pan and set aside.

3. Pour off all but 2 tablespoons of wine. Add olive oil, garlic, and red bell pepper to pan, and cook over medium-high heat for 5 minutes, stirring frequently. Add parsley, cooked prawns, and fettuccine. Toss well to reheat thoroughly and serve immediately.

Serves 4.

CALAMARI MARINARA WITH SPAGHETTI

If you've been reluctant to try calamari (the Italian name for squid) this versatile, economical dish might change your mind. The crushed tomatoes packed in tomato purée give the sauce plenty of body.

4 lb	squid, cleaned and skinned	1.8 kg
⅓ cup	olive oil	85 ml
4 cloves	garlic, minced	4 cloves
1 can (28 oz)	crushed tomatoes in purée	1 can (800 g)
1 tsp	dried oregano	1 tsp
1 tsp	dried basil	1 tsp
to taste	salt and freshly ground black pepper	to taste
¼ cup	chopped Italian parsley	60 ml
1 tsp	hot-pepper flakes	1 tsp
2 lb	spaghetti	900 g

1. Cut the squid crosswise into ¾-inch (1.9-cm) pieces. Cut the tentacles crosswise if they are large.

2. In a heavy casserole or Dutch oven, heat oil. Add squid and sauté for 5–6 minutes. Add garlic and stir for 1 minute. Add tomatoes, oregano, basil, salt, and pepper. Cover and allow to cook until squid are tender (about 20 minutes). Stir in parsley and hot-pepper flakes. Adjust seasonings to taste. Set aside.

3. Cook and drain pasta.

4. Pour sauce over pasta and serve hot or cold.

Serves 8.

Pasta with Smoked Salmon

Smoked salmon epitomizes elegance and luxury, but a little goes a long way in this recipe. Try using spinach pasta for an especially colorful dish.

1 ¼ lbs	fettuccine	570 g
4 oz	cream cheese	115 g
1 cup	milk	250 ml
¼ lb	sliced smoked salmon, cut into approximately ¼-inch (.6-cm) pieces	115 g
½ cup	cooked fresh or frozen tiny peas, thawed but not cooked	125 ml
2	green onions, including tops, finely sliced	2
2 tsp	lemon juice	2 tsp
1 tsp	finely chopped fresh dill or ¼ teaspoon dried	1 tsp
⅓ cup	freshly grated Parmesan cheese	85 ml

1. Cook and drain pasta. Set aside and keep warm.

2. In a medium saucepan combine cream cheese and milk. Heat, stirring, until mixture is smooth.

3. Stir in smoked salmon, peas, onion, lemon juice, and dill. Cook to heat through. Remove pan from heat. Stir in Parmesan cheese.

4. Toss sauce with cooked fettuccine and serve at once.

Serves 4 as a main dish or 6 as an appetizer.

PASTA SHELLS WITH FRESH PEAS AND CHICKEN

Small pasta shells baked with a sauté of red bell peppers, fresh peas, and slivers of skinned chicken breasts yield a low-fat main dish that can be made ahead of time.

3 cups	small shells	700 ml
2 cups	slivered cooked chicken, skinned	500 ml
2 tsp	olive oil	2 tsp
½ cup	fresh peas, shelled	125 ml
1 tbl	minced garlic	1 tbl
2 tbl	chopped fresh basil	2 tbl
1 tsp	dried thyme	1 tsp
3 tbl	chopped parsley	3 tbl
¼ cup	chopped red bell pepper	60 ml
¼ cup	grated Parmesan cheese	60 ml

1. Cook and drain pasta. Set aside.

2. Preheat oven to 400°F (205°C). In a large skillet over medium-high heat, sauté chicken in olive oil for 2 minutes; then add remaining ingredients except pasta and cheese. Cook 2 minutes more; then pour mixture into large baking dish. Add pasta shells and toss well. Add Parmesan cheese.

3. Bake for 20 minutes. Serve hot.

Serves 4.

ELEGANT PASTA MAIN COURSES

When an important occasion calls for an elegant entrée, think pasta. This section offers an uncommon collection of pasta main dishes for dinner parties, holidays, and other special events. With an impressive array of recipes ranging from time-honored Italian favorites to contemporary pasta specialties to choose from, you can pick the perfect pasta dish for any occasion.

FETTUCCINE WITH WILD MUSHROOMS

This memorable pasta dish combines classic techniques and choice ingredients.

1 lb	fettuccine	450 g
½ lb	fresh chanterelles or other wild mushrooms	225 g
2 cups	chicken stock	500 ml
1 tbl each	butter and oil	1 tbl each
2 tbl	minced green onions	2 tbl
¼ cup	dry white wine	60 ml
1½ cups	whipping cream	350 ml
to taste	salt and pepper	to taste
1 tbl	chopped parsley	1 tbl

1. Cook and drain pasta. Set aside and keep warm.

2. Brush debris off tops and undersides of mushrooms, discarding any damp, spongy parts. Save any dirty stems or caps, peel, and add to stock. Slice vertically through caps and stems to make pieces about ¼ inch (.6 cm) thick.

3. In a small saucepan bring stock to a boil. Cook over medium-high heat until reduced to about ½ cup (125 ml). Strain out peelings and discard.

4. In a large skillet heat butter and oil over medium-high heat. Add mushrooms and green onions and cook, stirring, until mushrooms begin to render liquid. Add wine and cook over high heat until liquid is mostly evaporated. Add reduced stock and cream and bring to a boil.

5. Reduce sauce to one half original volume and season with salt and pepper. Add cooked pasta and parsley to skillet, and toss to coat with sauce. Serve on warm plates.

Serves 4.

Fresh Pasta Primavera

This classic treat is a veritable garden on a plate.

¾ lb	angel hair	350 g
1 lb	sugar snap peas, strings removed	450 g
1 lb	fresh asparagus	450 g
1 cup	sliced slender green beans	250 ml
½ cup	thin carrot strips	125 ml
4 tbl	olive oil	4 tbl
2 tbl	unsalted butter	2 tbl
1 cup	diced red bell pepper	250 ml
2 tbl	pine nuts, toasted	2 tbl
1 cup	shredded romaine lettuce	250 ml
2 tbl	minced fresh chives	2 tbl
to taste	salt	to taste
4 tbl	minced fresh parsley, for garnish	4 tbl
as needed	freshly grated Parmesan cheese	as needed

1. Cook and drain pasta, reserving cooking water. Set cooked pasta aside and keep warm.

2. Bring water in which pasta was cooked to a boil. Blanch peas, asparagus, beans, and carrots separately, removing each batch to ice water as soon as it is tender but still crisp, to stop the cooking. Drain well and pat dry.

3. Heat the olive oil and butter in a large skillet over moderate heat. Add pepper and sauté one minute. Add pine nuts and sauté one more minute. Add blanched and drained peas, asparagus, beans, and carrots and toss until coated with oil and warmed through.

4. Place cooked pasta in a serving bowl. Add hot vegetables to pasta along with romaine and chives. Toss well, add salt to taste, and toss again. Garnish with minced parsley and pass grated Parmesan cheese separately.

Serves 4.

Red Pepper Pasta with Cilantro Sauce

Cilantro and red bell pepper marry tastefully in this elegantly light dish. Look for red bell pepper pasta in specialty stores or make your own, using roasted red bell peppers (see Designer Doughs on page 17).

Cilantro Sauce

4 cloves	garlic, finely minced	4 cloves
1 cup	walnuts, toasted and finely minced	250 ml
4 cups	parsley, minced	900 ml
1	lime or lemon, juiced	1
2 cups	cilantro (coriander leaves), minced	500 ml
⅓ cup	olive oil	85 ml
1½ tsp	salt	1½ tsp
4 oz	Asiago cheese, grated	115 g
2 lb	red bell pepper pasta	900 g
2 oz	Asiago cheese, grated	60 g

1. To prepare Cilantro Sauce, in a 2-quart (1.8-l) mixing bowl, stir to combine garlic, walnuts, parsley, lime juice, cilantro, oil, salt, and cheese. Set aside.

2. Cook and drain pasta. Toss pasta with Cilantro Sauce. Sprinkle with cheese and serve immediately.

Serves 8.

Gnocchi Garnishes

Besides making a satisfying main course or a side dish to accompany grilled chicken or roast meats, gnocchi are delicious as garnishes for any clear soup, such as sparkling consommé or well-flavored chicken stock. Delicately hued Gnocchi Verdi (see opposite page) make particularly handsome garnishes for light-colored broths or soups. For variety, cut the dough for gnocchi into diamonds or squares instead of making them round.

Gnocchi Verdi

A rich batter and fresh spinach are the essentials for classic Roman gnocchi. Serve as a side dish or in soup.

1 lb	fresh spinach (leaves only), washed thoroughly	450 g
¼ cup	butter	60 ml
¾ cup	cream cheese	175 ml
2	eggs, lightly beaten	2
2 tbl	whipping cream	2 tbl
½ cup	freshly grated Parmesan cheese	125 ml
¼ cup	unbleached flour	60 ml
to taste	salt and freshly ground black pepper	to taste

1. Put moist spinach leaves into a large sauté pan. Cover and cook, without adding extra water, until spinach is limp (about 5 minutes). Drain spinach thoroughly, pressing out any excess liquid; chop finely.

2. In the same skillet over medium heat, melt butter. Add spinach and cook until all moisture is evaporated, 2–3 minutes. Add cream cheese and cook, stirring constantly, to blend (about 5 minutes). Remove from heat and set aside.

3. In a small bowl combine eggs, cream, Parmesan cheese, and flour. Fold into spinach mixture in pan. Season with salt and pepper.

4. Pour batter into a shallow dish and spread into a thin layer. Cover and refrigerate until firm, at least 2 hours.

5. When ready to cook, use a spoon to shape batter into walnut-sized balls; set aside.

6. Bring a 4-quart (3.6-l) pot of salted water to a boil. Drop balls into water, reduce heat to medium-low, and simmer until they puff and rise to the surface. Remove with a slotted spoon and drain. Repeat until all batter has been used.

Makes about 25 gnocchi.

CRAB AND ARTICHOKE HEARTS WITH LEMON PASTA

Lemon-flavored pasta is a tangy contrast to succulent crab and artichoke hearts. This is a rich dish for special occasions.

1 recipe	Lemon Dough (see page 16)	1 recipe
3 cups	whipping cream	700 ml
½ cup	freshly grated Parmesan cheese	125 ml
½ cup	thinly sliced green onion, (use part of green)	125 ml
4½ oz	artichoke hearts, drained, rinsed, and chopped	125 g
2 cups	crabmeat, cooked	500 ml
¼ cup	unsalted butter, at room temperature	60 ml
to taste	salt and freshly ground black pepper	to taste

1. Prepare Lemon Dough and cut into linguine. Cook and drain pasta. Set aside and keep warm.

2. In medium pan heat cream and reduce until 1½ cups (350 ml) remain. Add ¼ cup (60 ml) of the Parmesan cheese, green onion, artichoke hearts, and crabmeat, and cook until just heated through.

3. Toss cooked pasta with the butter.

4. Pour the sauce over the buttered pasta and toss again. Sprinkle the remaining Parmesan cheese on top. Season with salt and pepper. Serve immediately.

Serves 4.

GINGERED MUSSELS WITH PASTA

This recipe combines Asian seasonings with creamy pasta.

2 lb	mussels, scrubbed and debearded	900 g
4 slices	fresh ginger	4 slices
2	shallots, finely chopped	2
2 cloves	garlic, finely chopped	2 cloves
½ cup	white wine	125 ml
1 lb	tagliarini	450 g
1½ tbl	olive oil	1½ tbl
1½ tbl	unsalted butter	1½ tbl
2 tbl	finely shredded fresh ginger	2 tbl
½ lb	medium shrimp, shelled and deveined	225 g
½ lb	small bay scallops	225 g
½ cup	heavy cream	125 ml
1–2 tsp	freshly squeezed lemon juice	1–2 tsp
½ tsp	salt	½ tsp
to taste	freshly ground black pepper	to taste
as needed	fresh watercress, for garnish	as needed

1. Place mussels in a steamer. Scatter ginger slices, shallot, and half the garlic on top and sprinkle with wine. Cover and steam over medium-high heat until mussels open, about 5 minutes. Discard ginger slices. Remove mussels and reserve; pour juices, including garlic and shallot, into a small saucepan. Cook over high heat until reduced to ½ cup (125 ml). Set aside.

2. Cook and drain pasta. Place on a warmed platter. Preheat wok over medium heat; when hot, pour in oil; then add butter. Add remaining garlic and shredded ginger and sauté until soft (about 30 seconds). Increase heat to medium-high; add shrimp and sauté until they just begin to turn pink, about 1 minute. Add scallops and toss. Add reserved reduced juices and cream; cook until sauce is reduced to a creamy consistency (about 1 minute). Add reserved mussels, lemon juice, salt, and pepper. Spoon over pasta. Garnish with watercress.

Serves 4.

Cannelloni Bolognese

Homemade cannelloni are worthy of the effort they require to make.

1 recipe	Classic Bolognese Sauce (see page 25)	1 recipe
1 recipe	Basic Egg Dough (see page 15)	1 recipe
1 recipe	Fresh Herb Dough (see page 17)	1 recipe

Balsamella Sauce

6 tbl	unsalted butter	6 tbl
1½ tbl	flour	1½ tbl
3 cups	milk	700 ml
⅓–½ cup	half-and-half	85–125 ml
1 tbl	sweet vermouth	1 tbl
pinch	nutmeg	pinch
to taste	salt and white pepper	to taste

Spinach and Cheese Filling

2 tbl	olive oil	2 tbl
2 tbl	minced shallot	2 tbl
2 tbl	minced carrot	2 tbl
4 bunches	fresh spinach, stemmed, leaves blanched, squeezed dry, and chopped	4 bunches
⅓ lb	prosciutto, sliced paper-thin and shredded	150 g
¾ lb	ricotta cheese	350 g
1 cup	freshly grated Parmesan cheese	250 ml
¼ cup	freshly grated mozzarella cheese	60 ml
2	eggs	2
1	egg yolk	1
to taste	salt and freshly ground black pepper	to taste
pinch	nutmeg	pinch
¼ cup	freshly grated Parmesan cheese	60 ml
3 tbl	unsalted butter, at room temperature	3 tbl

1. Prepare Classic Bolognese Sauce and set aside.

2. Prepare Basic Egg Dough and Fresh Herb Dough and set aside.

3. To prepare Balsamella sauce, in a 1½-quart (1.4-l) saucepan over moderate heat, melt 4 tablespoons of the butter. Add flour and cook, stirring, for 5 minutes. Gradually add milk in a slow, steady stream, whisking constantly. Cook over medium heat 20 minutes, stirring occasionally. Stir in ⅓ cup (85 ml) of the half-and-half, vermouth, nutmeg, and salt and pepper to taste. Continue cooking about 15 minutes, or until sauce is thick and smooth. If sauce thickens too much, add a little more half-and-half. Whisk in remaining butter. Taste and adjust seasoning. Set aside to cool.

4. To prepare Spinach and Cheese Filling, heat olive oil in a large skillet over moderate heat. Add shallot and carrot; sauté 3 minutes. Remove from heat. Stir in spinach, prosciutto, ricotta, Parmesan, mozzarella, eggs, and egg yolk. Season to taste with salt, pepper, and nutmeg, and set aside.

5. Roll pasta into sheets. Cut into 16 rectangles approximately 3 by 4 inches (7.5 by 10 cm). Bring a large pot of salted water to a boil. Parboil pasta in batches for 10 seconds. Remove with a slotted spoon and refresh in ice water. Drain and dry thoroughly. Arrange atop clean dish towels. Top with clean dish towels and set aside.

6. Preheat oven to 350°F (175°C). Spoon 3 tablespoons of filling on each pasta rectangle. Roll up into a neat tube. Spread 1 cup (250 ml) of Balsamella Sauce over bottom of an ovenproof casserole, approximately 11 by 14 inches (27.5 by 35 cm). Arrange cannelloni in the casserole side by side, alternating egg and herb rolls. Top with Classic Bolognese and remaining Balsamella sauces. Dust with Parmesan cheese, dot with butter, cover with foil, and bake 10 minutes. Uncover; bake 10 minutes more to brown the top. Serve immediately.

Serves 8.

Ravioli with Cheese Filling

These plump little pillows filled with mozzarella are topped with a traditional Italian tomato sauce.

2 recipes	Basic Egg Dough (see page 15)	2 recipes
1 recipe	Northern Italian Tomato Sauce (see page 22)	1 recipe

Cheese Filling

3 tbl	olive oil	3 tbl
1 tbl	butter	1 tbl
3 tbl	minced leek	3 tbl
½ tbl	minced garlic	½ tbl
1 tsp	dried oregano	1 tsp
2 tbl	Marsala	2 tbl
2 tbl	whipping cream	2 tbl
¼ cup	ricotta cheese	60 ml
¼ cup	grated mozzarella cheese	60 ml
to taste	salt and freshly ground black pepper	to taste
pinch	nutmeg	pinch
3 tbl	minced parsley, for garnish	3 tbl
¼ cup	freshly grated Parmesan cheese, for garnish	60 ml

1. Prepare dough and Northern Italian Tomato Sauce. Set aside.

2. To prepare Cheese Filling, heat oil and butter in a skillet over moderate heat. When butter foams, add leek and garlic. Sauté gently until leek is very soft (about 15 minutes). Add oregano and sauté 2 minutes. Add Marsala, turn heat up to high, and cook until Marsala is almost completely evaporated. Reduce heat to medium and add cream. Stir to combine; simmer until cream thickens into a sauce (about 2–3 minutes). Remove from heat and cool slightly. Stir in cheeses; season to taste with salt, pepper, and nutmeg. Set aside.

3. Prepare ravioli, following directions on page 84.

4. Bring a large pot of salted water to a boil. Add ravioli to boiling water a few at a time; do not crowd the pot. Ravioli will sink, then float. After they begin to float, cook 2½ minutes. Remove one and taste for doneness. With a slotted spoon, remove cooked ravioli to a platter and keep warm in a low oven. Add remaining ravioli to boiling water in batches until all are cooked.

5. Reheat sauce. When all ravioli are on the platter, top with hot sauce. Garnish with parsley and Parmesan cheese.

Serves 4 to 6.

PREPARING RAVIOLI

Ravioli can be made with a variety of doughs and fillings. Use any of the pasta doughs on pages 15–18. The dough and filling should be compatible in flavor and color.

The dough should be rolled quite thin. Using a mold to form the ravioli simplifies the process, but is not essential. Ravioli can be prepared a few hours ahead of serving time and spread on lightly floured baking sheets. Make sure they do not touch.

Cover and refrigerate or freeze. Place in a lock-top plastic bag and use within three months. After cooking, ravioli can be added to broth or sauced with Fresh Tomato and Herb Sauce (see page 24) or Parmigiano Cream Sauce (see page 31).

1. Roll pasta dough into thin sheets. Place mounds of filling, about ¾ teaspoon each, at regular intervals the length of the pasta. Brush lightly with cold water between the mounds.

2. Place another sheet of pasta over the first and use your fingers to press sheets together between the mounds of filling.

3. Cut ravioli with a pizza cutter or pastry wheel. Use a fork to crimp and seal the edges.

LOWFAT LASAGNE

Luscious and *pleasingly low in fat, this main dish is inexpensive and easy to prepare.*

1½ recipe	Northern Italian Tomato Sauce (see page 22)	1½ recipe
1 lb	spinach lasagne	450 g
2 cups	sliced onions	500 ml
2 cups	sliced mushrooms	500 ml
1 cup	white wine	250 ml
2 cups	chopped spinach leaves	500 ml
1 tsp	salt	1 tsp
1 cup	crumbled firm tofu	250 ml
1 cup	part-skim ricotta cheese	250 ml
as needed	oil, for greasing baking dish	as needed
2 tbl	Parmesan cheese	2 tbl
¼ cup	bread crumbs	60 ml

1. Prepare Northern Italian Tomato Sauce and set aside. Cook and drain pasta and set aside.

2. Sauté onions and mushrooms in white wine over medium heat until soft (about 10 minutes). Add spinach leaves and salt and cook, covered, for 1 minute. Remove from heat and mix with tofu and ricotta. Set aside.

3. Preheat oven to 375°F (190°C). Lightly oil a 9- by 12-inch (22.5- by 30-cm) baking dish.

4. Assemble lasagne by layering spinach filling, sauce, and lasagne. Repeat twice, using all ingredients and ending with lasagne on top.

5. Mix Parmesan cheese and bread crumbs and sprinkle on top of lasagne. Bake for 30 minutes.

Serves 6 to 8.

Lasagne con Tre Formaggi

This lasagne makes a fancy accompaniment to ham or pork roast.

6 oz	lasagne	170 g
2 recipes	Parmigiano Cream Sauce (see page 31)	2 recipes
4 tbl	olive oil	4 tbl
2	shallots, minced	2
1 bunch	spinach, washed and shredded	1 bunch
3 lb	ricotta cheese	1.4 kg
2	tomatoes, sliced	2
1 lb	mozzarella cheese, sliced	450 g
1 cup	parsley, minced	250 ml

1. Cook and drain pasta and set aside. Prepare Parmigiano Cream Sauce and set aside.

2. Grease an 8- by 12-inch (20- by 30-cm) baking dish with 2 tablespoons of the olive oil. Preheat oven to 350°F (175°C). In a 12-inch (30-cm) skillet over low heat, heat remaining olive oil. Sauté shallots and spinach together until spinach is wilted (about 8 minutes).

3. Place ½ cup (125 ml) Parmigiano Sauce in baking dish. Place one layer of lasagne on sauce. For first layer: Spread 1 pound (450 g) ricotta on lasagne, cover with one half the tomato, then ½ cup (125 ml) Parmigiano Sauce, and another layer of lasagne. For next layer: Spread 1 pound (450 g) ricotta on lasagne, cover with all of spinach mixture, one half of the mozzarella, another ½ cup (125 ml) Parmigiano Sauce, and top with another layer of lasagne. For the final layer: Spread on remaining ricotta, remaining tomato, remaining mozzarella, ½ cup (125 ml) Parmigiano Sauce, and remaining lasagne. Top with remaining Parmigiano Sauce and sprinkle with parsley.

4. Bake until lightly browned on top and bubbly around edges (about 35 minutes). Cool 10 minutes before serving.

Serves 8.

PASTA PRIMADONNA

A lean variation on Fresh Pasta Primavera, this version is made with either whole wheat or spinach pasta and baked in a lowfat sauce.

Primadonna Sauce

2 tsp	butter	2 tsp
2 tsp	flour	2 tsp
1 cup	milk	250 ml
⅓ cup	grated Parmesan cheese	85 ml
¼ tsp	white pepper	¼ tsp
8 oz	whole wheat or spinach pasta	225 g
as needed	oil, for greasing baking dish	as needed
¼ cup	dry sherry	60 ml
1 tsp	olive oil	1 tsp
⅓ cup	chopped green onion	85 ml
1 tsp	minced garlic	1 tsp
1	red bell pepper, seeded and chopped	1
¼ tsp	ground cumin	¼ tsp
½ tsp	dried oregano	½ tsp
1 tbl	chopped fresh basil	1 tbl
½ cup	asparagus, cut diagonally into 2-inch (5-cm) lengths	125 ml
1 cup	cherry tomatoes, halved	250 ml
½ cup	whole snow peas, trimmed	125 ml

1. To prepare Primadonna Sauce, in a saucepan heat butter and stir in flour. Cook 2 minutes, stirring, to eliminate floury taste; then slowly add milk, stirring with a whisk. If milk is added slowly enough, the sauce should thicken to a heavy cream consistency. Add cheese and pepper and set aside.

2. Preheat oven to 400°F (205°C). Cook and drain pasta. Place in a large bowl and set aside.

3. Lightly grease a large baking dish. In a skillet heat sherry and olive oil and sauté green onion, garlic, and bell pepper until

pepper is soft but not mushy. Add remaining ingredients and sauté 2 minutes, stirring frequently.

4. Remove from heat and toss with pasta and Primadonna Sauce. Spoon into baking dish. Bake until lightly browned and bubbling (about 25 minutes).

Serves 4 to 6.

DESSERT PASTAS

Sweet pasta dishes are nothing new: A baked pudding-like pasta dish made with fettuccine has long been an Eastern European specialty; a soufflé incorporating vermicelli is a classic French dessert; and in India vermicelli cooked with a delicately spiced and sweetened cream sauce is popular. On the following pages you'll find a medley of creative confections that eloquently demonstrate how pasta makes the perfect finale to a meal.

Chocolate Fettuccine with Raspberries

This stunning dessert has a sophisticatedly subtle flavor.

1½ cups	heavy cream	350 ml
4–6 tbl	confectioners' sugar	4–6 tbl
2 cups	flour	500 ml
1 cup	cocoa powder	250 ml
½ cup	sugar	125 ml
¼ tsp	cinnamon	¼ tsp
pinch	salt	pinch
3	eggs, slightly beaten	3
1 tbl	olive oil	1 tbl
¼ tsp	vanilla extract	¼ tsp
1 pint	raspberries	500 ml
as needed	cocoa powder, for garnish	as needed

1. Whip cream until it falls in soft (not stiff) peaks when dropped from a spoon. Fold in confectioners' sugar to taste. Set aside.

2. Place flour, cocoa powder, sugar, cinnamon, and salt in bowl. Stir to blend. Lightly blend eggs, oil, and vanilla together. Mix ingredients and knead by hand or by machine (see instructions on pages 19–21). Cut dough to form fettuccine or your favorite flat pasta variety. Dry dough for 10–15 minutes.

3. Cook and drain pasta, shaking briskly to drain off cooking water. Divide pasta among 4 warmed dessert plates and scatter raspberries over pasta, reserving a dozen raspberries for garnish. Top each serving of pasta with ¾ cup (175 ml) sweetened whipped cream. Dust with cocoa powder and garnish with reserved raspberries. Serve at once.

Note *If the dough seems too dry, add water (no more than ½ teaspoon at a time) to moisten until dough is of the proper consistency. If the dough seems too moist, add a mixture of flour and cocoa powder (no more than 1 tablespoon at a time).*

Serves 4.

CANNELLONI WITH HOT FUDGE SAUCE

This shamelessly sweet version of traditional cannelloni is worth the effort it takes to prepare. If you're pressed for time, use packaged cannelloni and substitute bottled chocolate sauce or strawberry or other fruit syrup for the fudge sauce.

½ recipe	Basic Egg Dough (see page 15)	½ recipe
1 lb	mascarpone cheese	450 g
3 tbl	dark rum	3 tbl
¾ cup	sugar	170 g

Hot Fudge Sauce

6 tbl	unsalted butter	6 tbl
½ cup	water	125 ml
4 oz	unsweetened chocolate	115 g
1 cup	sugar	250 ml
3 tbl	light corn syrup	3 tbl
⅛ tsp	salt	⅛ tsp
2 tsp	vanilla extract	2 tsp
as desired	strawberries, for garnish	as desired

1. Prepare Basic Egg Dough and make cannelloni as directed on pages 80–81. Cook and drain pasta and set aside.

2. Mix mascarpone cheese, rum, and sugar. Fill prepared cannelloni as directed on page 81.

3. To prepare Hot Fudge Sauce, in a heavy-bottomed 1-quart (900-ml) saucepan, melt butter in the water over medium heat. Bring to a boil, stirring constantly. Add chocolate, stirring occasionally, until it melts. (Do not worry if chocolate lumps at this point; it will smooth out later.) Add sugar, corn syrup, and salt. Boil 5 minutes. Remove from heat and add vanilla.

4. Drizzle heated Hot Fudge Sauce over filled cannelloni and garnish with strawberries.

Serves 4.

ALSATIAN POPPY SEED PASTA

This dessert is a sweet variation on a popular Alsatian dish. Toasting the poppy seeds to a fragrant crispness in a dry skillet over low heat brings out their flavor.

½ lb	fresh or dried fettuccine	225 g
4 tbl	unsalted butter	4 tbl
4 tbl	whipping cream	4 tbl
1 tbl	poppy seed, lightly toasted	1 tbl
½ cup plus 2 tbl	sugar	125 ml plus 2 tbl
1 tsp	vanilla	1 tsp

1. Cook and drain pasta and set aside.

2. In a 12-inch (30-cm) skillet over moderately low heat, melt butter. Whisk in whipping cream, 2 teaspoons poppy seed, ½ cup (125 ml) of the sugar, and vanilla. Bring to a simmer and cook until well blended and slightly thickened (about 1 minute). Remove from heat.

3. Add pasta to sauce and stir to coat. Return skillet to moderately high heat and cook, stirring constantly, until hot throughout (about 1 minute). Transfer to a warm platter and top with the remaining poppy seed and the 2 tablespoons of sugar. Serve immediately.

Serves 4.

Raisin and Apple Kugel

This fruited pasta of German and Austrian origin appeals to anyone who prefers a satisfying dessert that isn't too sweet. Apples and raisins stud the layers of lasagne and creamy cheese in this dish.

8 oz	lasagne	225 g
as needed	oil, for baking dish	as needed
2 tsp	melted butter	2 tsp
2 tbl	honey	2 tbl
2 tbl	Neufchâtel cheese	2 tbl
1 cup	cottage cheese	250 ml
1 cup	plain yogurt	250 ml
2 tbl	cinnamon	2 tbl
1 tsp	salt	1 tsp
2	egg whites, beaten	2
2	whole eggs, beaten	2
½ cup	raisins	125 ml
3	red or golden Delicious apples, cored and sliced thin	3
⅓ cup	milk	85 ml
¼ cup	brown sugar	60 ml

1. Cook and drain pasta. Set aside.

2. Preheat oven to 400°F (205°C). Lightly oil a 9- by 12-inch (22.5- by 30-cm) baking dish.

3. In a mixing bowl combine butter, honey, Neufchâtel, cottage cheese, yogurt, cinnamon, salt, egg whites, and whole eggs. In another bowl combine raisins and apples.

4. Layer kugel by alternating cheese mixture, pasta, and fruit mixture, ending with pasta. Pour milk over the top. Sprinkle brown sugar on top.

5. Bake for 40 minutes; then let cool and slice into squares.

Serves 8.

Index